A

CHURCH

in

MOTION

Published by:

Clear Faith Publishing LLC
22 Lafayette Rd
Princeton, NJ 08540

ISBN 978-1-940414-04-1

Printed in the United States of America

First Printing September, 2015
Cover and Interior Design by Doug Cordes
A Church in Motion is typeset in Paperback

Contact Information

261 City Ave.
Merion Station, PA 19066-1835
610-660-1424; wbyron@sju.edu

A

CHURCH

in

MOTION

Reflections on
CONTEMPORARY
CATHOLIC LIFE

WILLIAM J. BYRON, S.J.

Dedicated to my

GRANDNIECES AND GRANDNEPHEWS:

Christina, Billy, and Emily;

Cassie and Joe;

Martita;

Lily and Nicholas

Table of Contents

========   *Introduction*   ========

This small book was a joy to assemble.

All of it is original with me, of course, but much of it saw the light of print earlier on in my bi-weekly column, "Looking Around," distributed by the Catholic News Service syndicate. Ideas on the Sunday obligation, preaching, and the danger of the "Catholic Salt Losing Its Savor" appeared in the pages of *The Priest Magazine*, a service to the Church provided by Our Sunday Visitor Publishing.

What you hold in your hand is a window into our contemporary Catholic world. It is not the world into which I was born, Baptized, and later ordained for service as a priest. But it is the world in which my nieces and nephews and their children—the grandnieces and grandnephews mentioned in the dedication—are living their Catholic lives. I don't claim to provide comprehensive coverage here; I simply want to offer observations and reflections which may stimulate further thought and discussion among those who are walking the way of faith today—the Catholic faith—into an unknown future.

WJB
St. Joseph's University
Philadelphia, PA

Chapter One

EXTENDING THE PERIMETERS
OF THE PAPACY

Early in the 21st century, the Holy Spirit showed signs of being alive and well in the Roman Catholic Church. A pope resigned. A surprising successor was elected. And the eyes of the world turned to Rome.

FAREWELL TO BENEDICT.

The timing of Pope Benedict's resignation was just right. When Joseph Ratzinger was elected Pope in 2005 at age 78, I was working at Loyola College (now University) in Baltimore. A local radio announcer, who was on the air during the late afternoon commute, telephoned me to discuss this breaking news with him on the air. "He's a little old for the job, isn't he?, asked the call-in host, who had never met me before. "He's exactly one month older than I am," I replied.

"Well, I have to say he looked pretty good there on television dressed all in white when he stepped out onto that balcony," the radio host remarked a bit defensively. "And did you know he was in the German army and a prisoner of war in the Second World War?" he asked. "I may have guarded him," I said, just to pull the announcer's leg a bit; "I was in the U.S. Army in Germany at that time," although Ratzinger the soldier had slipped away from military service just before I arrived in his homeland as part of the Army of Occupation after Germany surrendered in 1945.

I was happy to hear in February 2013 that Pope Benedict decided to resign at age 85. He deserved some downtime after eight years in a terribly demanding job. He was making an important point for the entire world to see; this was namely that the papacy is a function, not a person, and that an organization as large and complex as the 1.2 billion-member Roman Catholic Church needs vigor as well as holiness and intelligence at the top.

The mission of the Church, Pope Benedict often said, is to proclaim the Good News. This proclamation has to be not only faithful, but enthusiastic. Add to this the need for creativity and mobility in proclaiming the Good News, and you don't have far to travel to reach the conclusion that, in this case, the timing was just right.

When he addressed Catholic educators here in the U.S. in 2008, Pope Benedict noted a "reluctance" on the part of many moderns to entrust themselves to God. Entrusting oneself to God involves an act of the will, and this, he said, is a "complex phenomenon and one which I ponder continually." Well, that pondering brought him to conclude that it was time to entrust the Church to new leadership, and himself to the God who holds his destiny in his hands. If leading by example is still a worthy objective, and who would argue that it is not, we have here an instance of exemplary leadership for the whole world to see. And the world did indeed take notice.

History will, I suspect, judge Pope Benedict's papacy kindly. His service to the Church will continue now in unseen, yet not insignificant ways. The Cardinals, gathered in Rome to size each other up with a view to papal succession, did their Church a great service by reminding themselves that servant leadership is what the Church needs now more than ever. It is the model given to us by Jesus, "who came not to be served, but to serve and to give his life as a ransom for many" (Mark 10:45). The world began watching to see how close Benedict's successor, Pope Francis, will come to meeting the demands of that job description.

NEW POPE, NEW ERA

As the world awaited word on who would be elected to succeed Pope Benedict XVI as leader of the Roman Catholic Church, there was much talk about the need for reform and transparency in the Vatican Curia, as well as the virtual impossibility of anyone who might be regarded as a Vatican insider being able to meet the challenge. Then, along with the white smoke also came the surprising news that the College of Cardinals had turned to Latin America and elected a native of Argentina, who happened also to be a Jesuit, to occupy the Chair of Peter.

The new Pope chose to take the name Francis, honoring the memory and legacy of St. Francis of Assisi, the Poverello, or 'poor one,' best loved of all the Saints, thus winning the hearts of countless Catholics worldwide who admire Franciscan spirituality. He gave no indication of doing so, but Jorge Mario Bergoglio might also have adopted the familiar and famous Prayer of St. Francis as a 'mission statement' for his papal ministry.

"Lord, make me an instrument of your peace; where there is hatred, let me sow love; where there is injury, pardon; where there is doubt, faith; where there is despair, hope; where there is darkness, light; and where there is sadness, joy." This is exactly what the world needs now!

Commentators all over the world associated the person and style of the new Pope with the simplicity, humility, and forgiveness of the words. Upon becoming Archbishop of Buenos Aires in 1998, he chose not to live in the archbishop's mansion, gave up the car and driver, chose to take public transportation to work, and cooked his own meals all while living in a small apartment. Talk about setting a good example for the clergy!

He began right away to bring transparency and much-needed reform into the Vatican Curia—the governing bureaucracy. He speaks Italian fluently and has had experiences of service on several Vatican congregations, although he has never lived in Rome as a full-time Vatican bureaucrat. This brings me back to the immediate challenge awaiting him—reform of the Vatican Curia.

In the early 1970's when I was named Dean of Arts and Sciences at Loyola University in New Orleans, which is located immediately next door to Tulane University, I decided to visit my counterpart at Tulane, an 18-year veteran of the academic deanship there, to get acquainted and seek some advice. His opening words to me were, "You're going to find that it would be easier to move a cemetery than to move a liberal arts faculty."

I thought of those words as I looked at Pope Francis on television, smiling and waving to well- wishers from the balcony overlooking St. Peter's Square. Before blessing them, he asked for their blessing and their prayers. He'll need them as he shoulders the job of moving the cemetery. Both figuratively and practically speaking, there is no more difficult archaeological terrain anywhere in the world than in Rome for doing just that.

In order to maintain the new era of transparency and reform within the Vatican, Pope Francis will need all of the prayers that he can get.

IT'S A MOVEMENT, NOT A MONUMENT

The overwhelmingly positive worldwide response to the person, example, and message of Pope Francis, well after he settled into his papacy, serves as a reminder that Christianity is a movement and not a monument.

It all began when a charismatic young man left his hometown of Nazareth, and started to walk country roads and shorelines inviting others to follow him. He asked fishermen to drop their nets and respond to his invitation to become fishers of men and women. He preached Good News of Salvation, and established his credentials by miraculous actions and compassionate care for those in need.

At the beginning of his public ministry, as Luke's Gospel relates it, Jesus returned "to Nazareth, where he had grown up, and went according to his custom into the synagogue on the Sabbath day. He stood up to read and was handed a scroll of the prophet Isaiah." Jesus then unrolled the scroll and read these famous words: "The Spirit of the Lord is upon me, because he has anointed me to bring glad tidings to the poor. He has sent me to proclaim liberty to captives and recovery of sight to the blind, to let the oppressed go free, and to proclaim a year acceptable to the Lord." After reading those words, he said to all present, "Today this Scripture passage is fulfilled in your hearing."

Thus the movement began. Eventually, however, over the centuries the movement hardened into a monument of hierarchical structure, ecclesiastical rules and regulations, and architectural rigidities. This is not to say that structure isn't necessary. If anyone reading this book did not have a bone structure, he or she would be a puddle of flesh plopped on the floor. Nor can a worldwide community of 1.2 billion believers live without some rules and regulations. Of course, if believers are expected to remember their Lord in the breaking of the bread, they have to have some place, some sacred space, where they can assemble and worship.

But rigidities of rank, rule, and building construction can cripple the movement and replace it with monumental cathedrals, chancery offices, rectories, a promotion culture, and brick-and-mortar barriers that prevent the flow of loving people and liberating ideas which Jesus launched.

By taking the name Francis, the Holy Father signaled his desire to see the values of Francis of Assisi, the Poverello, surface as defining characteristics of this movement called Christianity. By paying his own hotel bill at the end of the conclave that elected him to the Chair of Peter, and by choosing to live in simple quarters rather than a papal palace, Pope Francis said 'No' to privilege and 'Yes' to the lifestyle adopted by the Son of Man who came, "not to be served, but to serve, and to give his life for the ransom of many" (Mark 10:45).

His words and actions have caught the attention of a world in need of the simplicity for which he offers witness consistently and cheerfully. The world appears to be saying 'Amen' to what he has to offer.

A GLIMPSE INTO THE MIND OF POPE FRANCIS

In the self-revelatory interview of Pope Francis published by several Jesuit journals around the world in September 2013, the Holy Father mentioned that he had read Allesandro Manzoni's 1828 novel *The Betrothed* three times and had it on a nearby table for a fourth reading whenever the opportunity presented itself. That was 'three times and looking forward to a fourth'—that's a recommendation to be taken seriously! It prompted me to pick up the book and give it a read; one way, I thought, of getting inside the mind of this fascinating pope.

The point of mentioning this here is not to repeat the recommendation. It is not an easy read—605 pages that tell a long and involved love story in a Catholic world that no longer exists and takes the reader through war and plague and emotional hardship on the way to a happy ending. Manzoni (1785-1873) was the principal novelist of 19th century Italy, and this work is considered the greatest Italian novel of modern times.

The troubles of the betrothed peasant couple, Renzo and Lucia, are rooted in the cowardice of a parish priest who is intimidated by a local baron. In turn, the baron has his lustful eye on the innocent Lucia, and he forces the timid priest to delay the marriage.

A confrontation (a few hundred pages later) between the comfort-seeking, self-serving priest and his Cardinal may provide the key to the obvious fascination which Pope Francis has with this story.

"Father, why did you not marry that poor girl Lucia to her betrothed?" The question drew stammers, evasions, and nothing that could serve as a defensible answer, even the admission that the baron's opposition "forbade me to carry out the marriage under pain of death."

"And does that seem a sufficient reason to you not to carry out a definite duty?", replied the cardinal, who then goes on to say: "[D]on't you realize that suffering for the cause of justice is our way of conquering? If you do not know this, what is it you preach? What are the good tidings you have to announce to the poor? Does anyone expect you to conquer might by might? You will certainly never be asked one day if you have managed to check the strong; for you were not given either the mission or the means for that. But you will assuredly be asked if you have used the means you had at your disposal to do what was prescribed, even when anyone was rash enough to try and stop you."

"And why. . . have you bound yourself to a ministry which pledges you to a continual struggle with the passions of the world? . . . [W]hy. . . have you forgotten that whenever you need courage to carry out your obligations in this ministry, however you started in it, there is One who will give it infallibly to you if you but ask for it? Do you think that all those millions of martyrs were courageous by nature?"

As I said, I thought that by reading this book, I might get a glimpse into the mind of Pope Francis. I think that I did. It is a pleasure to see that mind, and the Gospel-rooted ideas it generates—at work in our world today.

Chapter Two

IS THE CATHOLIC SALT
LOSING ITS SAVOR?

Here is a question which needs to be asked as the Church moves deeper into the 21st century: "Is the Catholic salt losing its savor?"

The typical dictionary will tell you that 'salient' means conspicuous, standing out, significant, or prominent. 'Salience' suggests that a given topic is noteworthy. The word offers a hint that there is something appetizing or tasty associated with the matter at hand.

Sociologists speak of the 'salience of religion' as an indicator of religiosity, or the depth of religious commitment in a person or group. If they use a questionnaire in searching for the importance of religion in a person's life, they will typically ask: "How important would you say that religion is to you?" They usually scale the possible answers in this order: Extremely important, quite important, fairly important, not too important, or not important at all. If they attempt to measure religiosity *quantitatively*, *then* they will ask about the frequency of prayer and the regularity of attendance at worship services.

There is a notable decline in the salience of religion in the American mind as we move along in the 21st century. There is also a measurable drop in the Sunday worship and participation rates of Catholic community members, particularly among the young. We Catholics have a formidable challenge on our hands.

First, we have to recognize that something is wrong, and next, we have to do something about it. In doing something about it, we have to look first at ourselves, and not at those who are no longer showing up for services.

THE SALT OF THE EARTH

To put this within a Scriptural context, turn to the Sermon on the Mount where Jesus says: "You are the salt of the earth. But if salt loses its taste, with what can it be seasoned? It is no longer good for anything but to be thrown out and trampled underfoot" (Matthew 5:13).

We should open our ears, our minds, and our hearts to the reality that in our midst, in our day, the Catholic salt is losing its savor and it is up to us in varying degrees to guard what's left from being trampled underfoot. Priests have to assume a leadership responsibility for turning things around, of course. That's what they were ordained to do. But laypersons have to be a part of this effort, as well.

The etymological link between salt—the Latin word for which is *sal*—and 'salience' is obvious. So we have to wonder how and why we've managed in recent years to stand by idly (despite our so-called 'Year of Faith' and all our talk about the 'New Evangelization'); we have to wonder why we seem to be standing by idly as the salt of Catholic practice (measured, for example, in Sunday Mass attendance) is losing its savor.

I've been thinking a lot lately about published reports of fewer Catholics showing up for Mass on Sundays, and some of them checking out of the Church altogether. I wonder whether or not those who leave miss the Eucharist. This raises the question of the effectiveness of Catholic catechesis relative to the centrality of Eucharist to Catholic life.

What does the 'real presence' of Christ in the Eucharist really mean? If it means anything at all, why are growing numbers of Catholics saying, in effect, "No thanks; not interested?"

Christ is present to us in the Eucharistic liturgy in four ways: 1—in his Word, 2—in his Body and Blood, 3—in the worshipping community (as Jesus said, "whenever two or three are gathered in my name, I'm there in their midst"), and 4—in the presence of the priest through whose ministry Christ now offers what he originally offered on the Cross.

These four modes of Christ's presence in the Eucharistic liturgy are, to say the least, insufficiently understood and vastly underappreciated in Catholic worshipping assemblies today. This four-way real presence should be a four-way stop sign halting the exodus which researchers are tracking and journalists are reporting about the Catholic Church.

For the good of the Church, catechetical repair work is needed. Pastoral attention has to be paid to this problem. Priests, bishops, deacons, and lectors can 'proclaim,' but they and many others must also 'explain' the four-way presence of Christ in the Eucharist.

It takes faith, of course, to see Christ where only bread and wine are visible, but that's what faith does for the believer. It gives sight where vision fails.

Priests have to work with wafers—not an easy task. They use wine, but many of the faithful never see it or taste it. So it is not easy to get at the reality underlying the signs of wafer-like bread and un-tasted wine, namely, the Body and Blood of Jesus.

Similarly, it will take a lot of faith for the people to see Jesus in the person of an unsmiling priest or bishop, even those who try to make themselves more presentable at the altar (I call them the weightwatchers), and try as well to make themselves less unworthy of their calling to serve the faithful by offering sacrifice. Some laypersons, with the appropriate equipment and skills, might volunteer to videotape a priest-presider and sit down with him for a video replay of how he looks at the altar and in the pulpit. Does he, for example, maintain eye contact with the people? Does he really 'celebrate' or just routinely 'read' the Mass? He might also benefit from the remark that one Catholic observer made recently: "There is no shortage of priests in the United States, but there is a serious shortage of celebrants."

THE MASS AS MEAL

The sacrifice of the Mass is also a meal. Worshippers have to attend to their role to gather around the table with their priest, not as isolated worshippers, but as brothers and sisters in the Lord who recognize Christ in one another and in the Breaking of the Bread. Priests have to summon people out of their isolation, get them to the table, and keep them engaged.

At the Last Supper, Jesus said to his disciples, in effect: "This is how I want you to remember me—as bread broken and passed around, as a cup poured out. And this is how I want all of you to relate to one another—as bread broken for the nourishment of others, as a cup poured out in generous service."

Every priest has to ask himself, "To what extent am I being broken and passed around for the nourishment of others? To what extent am I letting myself be poured out in generous service? To what extent is mine a 'poured out' life?" All who gather for the celebration of the Eucharist, all who receive Holy Communion, have to be asking themselves the same exact questions. Our attempt to give honest answers to those questions will inevitably open the door to questions about how we are living our lives, how we are managing our wealth and property, how we are caring for or neglecting the poor and needy. Pope Francis is offering the whole Church good leadership in this regard. It is time for the followership to get engaged.

Are we up to the challenge? That's for us to decide.

Chapter Three

THANKSGIVING AND THE SUNDAY OBLIGATION

All Americans are familiar with Thanksgiving Day; we welcome the return of this great tradition every November. It is a secular holiday, rather than a religious feast day. Thanksgiving puts the accent where it should be—on giving, saying, and giving thanks. For men and women of faith, God comes to mind first and foremost for expressions of gratitude when celebrating Thanksgiving Day. We Catholics do this at Mass every day, particularly on each Sunday. We know where to look when we want to give thanks!

Everyone knows what 'much obliged'—that expression from the old American vernacular—means. It says simply and directly, 'thank you.' That's what Catholics do whenever they celebrate Eucharist. Eucharist means 'thank you.' It is a thanks-saying, a thanks-giving, a liturgical thanks-doing that brings us before the Lord in gratitude as we express our thanks for the great gift of Salvation in Jesus Christ. And for Salvation, of course, we are all indeed much obliged.

Whenever we put ourselves in the thanks-saying, thanks-giving, thanks-doing mood, it is a good idea to pay attention to a rising sense of entitlement in America, especially among the young, along with the decline in Sunday Mass attendance on the part of the young. I'm convinced that ingratitude has something to do with this. Ingratitude is the very infrastructure of entitlement.

Moreover, entitlement has become our cultural condition here in the affluent society. We think that we deserve everything which we have. Entitlement prompts us to make demands, not to give thanks.

St. Ignatius of Loyola once remarked that "ingratitude is at the root of all sinfulness." He was on to something. When ingratitude takes over one's outlook, there is an erosion of the sense of obligation, including moral obligation, not to mention what we used to call the Sunday obligation. 'Much obliged,' as I indicated, is a way the old American vernacular had of saying thanks. But if you have nothing to be thankful for—i.e., if you consider yourself to be entitled to everything you have or might receive—you are unencumbered by a sense of any obligation. You are free to be your selfish, solipsistic, narcissistic self. Sadly, we notice a lot of selfishness and narcissism surrounding us in America today.

Total self-absorption is another word for sin. As St. Ignatius of Loyola pointed out, ingratitude is at the root of all sinfulness, of all self-absorption.

A quarter of a century ago, I found myself describing students, whom I was then meeting in the college classroom, as characterized by a sense of entitlement. They thought they *deserved* good grades, good health, good jobs, and the best of everything that the world had to offer. Cultural reinforcement for this attitude of entitlement came, and continues to come, through entertainment and advertising. The young think they have cures for all their ills, protections from all dangers, solutions for all their problems, answers (with or without the help of a search engine) to all their questions. It is all within reach. It is theirs for the taking. No need to say please. No need to say thanks.

This outlook has seeped down into high school and middle school minds—to the teens and tweens who never say thanks. Anyone who is caught in a culture of entitlement has some digging out to do. That work begins with some thoughts about faith-based gratitude.

Many years ago, I pressed a child for a working definition of the word 'gift.' It was Christmas Day, in fact, and she was my niece and we were gathered in the family room where gifts and their wrappings had been strewn around all over the place. "What's a gift?", I asked. "A gift is when somebody gives you something," this youngster said. I responded, "What if you had loaned me a dollar last week, and now I'm giving it back. Here, take this dollar. Is that a gift?" "No," she immediately replied. "Well, it fits your definition; you told me that 'a gift is when somebody gives you something' and, here, I'm giving you a dollar." A moment's pondering prompted her then to say, "A gift is when you get something you don't deserve."

How true. This very truth can prompt an awareness of gratitude, which, in turn, can provide protection from the virus of entitlement. Life will be a good deal happier for everyone if we realize that the gifts we receive are not only undeserved, but, in the Christian view of things, that they are symbols to remind us of the gift of Salvation to which none of us has a claim except through our faith in Christ Jesus the Lord.

This brings me back to the Sunday obligation. This obligation is unintelligible, except in terms of gratitude. We Sunday Mass-goers should be acknowledging ourselves to be much obliged to give praise and thanks to God as we go to Mass on Sunday. That's what Sunday Mass is all about. Not to do so would be to be an ingrate. No one—not even the most self-centered young person—likes an ingrate. So instead of arguing with the young about their Sunday obligation, we should simply invite them to avoid being ingrates by being the grateful Christians they've been called to be. That means regarding themselves as much obliged—much obliged to give praise and thanks to God; much obliged to love one another as Christ loves them.

As I mentioned in the last chapter, at the Last Supper Jesus said to his disciples, in effect: "This is how I want you to remember me—as bread broken and passed around, as a cup poured out. This is how I want you to relate to one another—as bread broken for the nourishment of others, as a cup poured out in generous service."

Each of us should take a moment to put the following question to ourselves, and to the young people with whom we live: *Am I an ingrate? Or do I really consider myself to be much obliged?* In this, you have a clue to the true nature of the Sunday obligation.

AN ATTITUDE OF GRATITUDE

As an endnote, by no means an afterthought, let me emphasize the centrality of gratitude to a Catholic life. 'Always and everywhere' is a fairly comprehensive expression. Some might say it is dimensionless. I'm not setting out here to measure the immeasurable; I'm just suggesting that whoever composed the Preface to the Second Eucharistic Prayer expected Catholic worshippers to live in a state of gratitude, to be characteristically grateful. But, *always and everywhere?* That seems to be expecting more than any of us mere mortals is capable of doing.

"It is truly right and just, our duty and our Salvation, always and everywhere to give you thanks, Father Most Holy." It is indeed appropriate, and a duty as well, for all of us to be grateful, to give thanks to God. If not 'always and everywhere' in a quite literal sense, then we can, it seems to me, and should, the Church seems to be saying, cultivate within ourselves—mind, soul, and heart—an attitude of gratitude.

We all know people who are characteristically optimistic. We enjoy being around others who have a positive outlook on life. It is reassuring to know that those you love also love you, and they can be counted on to be there for you—always and everywhere—no matter what. They are always cheerful, always reliable, and always dependable. Why not always grateful? That's a goal worth setting for ourselves. And the 'always and everywhere' dimensions of that state of thankfulness may not be so out of reach as one might suspect.

Gratitude is bedrock and foundational, not just in religion and worship, but in the project of living a fully human life. The practice of our Catholic faith turns around the idea of gratitude. Eucharist is at the center of it all. Eucharist, as I've said, means thanks-giving, thanks-saying, thanks-doing. It's too bad that more of us do not cultivate this attitude of gratitude and permit thankfulness to emerge from within and shape both our outlook and behavior.

You cannot be simultaneously grateful and unhappy. Is all the unhappiness in the world an indicator of the enormity of our gratitude deficit? Personally and collectively, that problem is worth looking into.

As I indicated earlier, the old American vernacular used 'much obliged' as an expression of gratitude. Is declining Sunday Mass attendance in the American Catholic community an indication of an erosion of the sense of obligation, or of a loss of a sense of gratitude? Either way, something is missing. In my view, gratitude is the missing link. Make gratitude the center of your life and you will want to be at Mass every Sunday to express your thanks. The Church invites you to do that in the company of other faith-committed grateful persons.

Nobody likes an ingrate. If you are not liked as much as you would like, or if you don't like yourself as much as you should, the problem may be the absence of gratitude at the center of your life. The solution is relatively simple. Be grateful for the gift of life, and the gift of faith. Be grateful for the Sacraments, for family, friends, health, education, job and everything else that is yours. Recognize that all of this is a gift to you, and take to heart the life-changing conclusion which can be drawn from this kind of reflection: If you are fully human, all you can be is grateful.

TAKING ANOTHER LOOK AT THE
SUNDAY OBLIGATION

In recent years, I've been studying the decline in Sunday Mass attendance within the Catholic community. An old friend, who knew what I was up to, sent me a letter indicating that one of his philosophy professors from years ago at Notre Dame used to remark that "Catholics have lost the sense of what is at stake in life." My friend interpreted his professor to be saying that "maybe a large number of Catholics may not be spending eternity in God's presence." My correspondent then added, "Father, as you surely know, fire and brimstone might not only not be effective, but can become counter-productive; yet what is at stake for souls must be conveyed with urgency."

He was obviously thinking of the "Sunday obligation" and the heavy penalty that he, as a catechized Catholic, had been taught was attached to willful omission of that obligation. It was a capital crime, a mortal sin. Hence the need today to consider 'with urgency' what is at stake.

In responding to my friend, I reminded him that when we were boys we often heard the cowboys on the Saturday afternoon movies say, "Much obliged," when they wanted to express their gratitude. It was a way of saying 'thank you' in the old American vernacular. We mimicked the cowhands later that night at supper by saying, "Much obliged, Ma'am," when our mothers placed the mashed potatoes on the table.

In searching now for a persuasive and non-threatening way to explain how the Church (which, by the way, opposes capital punishment!) wants us to understand the Sunday obligation, it might be good to recall the old American vernacular.

What the Church expects of its members on Sunday—Resurrection Day, the first day of the week—is a formal liturgical expression of thanks. Eucharist means thanks-doing, thanks saying, thanksgiving.

We give thanks for the gift of our Salvation through the Death, Resurrection, and Ascension of Jesus. Not to meet this obligation—not to offer praise and thanks—is to be an ingrate. Moreover, we do this in community, not as isolated individuals, because that's how we've been ransomed, that's how we've been saved—in community. Finally, we do it in the Eucharistic community because the Eucharist, a thanksgiving ritual, forms us into the *One* Body of Christ.

Who wants to be seen as an ingrate in the eyes of the Lord? Some who are no longer going to Mass on Sundays may be willing to admit that they are sinners; nobody's perfect. But ingrates? There's a question that deserves a bit of thought.

As the weekend approaches, all Catholics should be asking themselves: *Am I an ingrate? Or do I really consider myself to be much obliged*? If so, get to Mass on Sunday and express your gratitude.

.

Chapter Four

THINKING THROUGH
THE IMPLICATIONS OF THE
YEAR OF FAITH

When the Year of Faith opened in October 2013, Pope Benedict XVI invited the whole Church into "a time of particular reflection and rediscovery of the faith." He later decided, as Chapter One recounts, to vacate the Chair of Peter and pursue his own reflection and rediscovery. The prayers of the entire Catholic world went with him on that journey, and his prayers were undoubtedly with the rest of us as we did our best to follow the faith into our own unknown future.

The Jesuit Superior, General Fr. Adolfo Nicolás, in response to Pope Benedict's invitation to a Year of Faith, asked Jesuits worldwide this question: "What lights, shadows, challenges, and opportunities do we see in our environment with regard to faith?" And he followed that question with another: "What operative role does faith actually play in my life: for example, in my work; in the way I deal with difficulties; in the way I use time, resources, energy?" And he then extended that question by asking: "What do

I experience as challenges or obstacles to faith, and what sustains and deepens my faith?"

Those questions are still worthy of consideration by all Catholics, and I'd like to provide some impetus for that reflection right here.

I think of religious faith as the act, the attitude, the mind-set by which we entrust ourselves to God. In my view, faith and trust are twins. There is content to faith, of course. We make statements about who God is and what God has done in Creation and throughout human history. But propositional faith and attitudinal faith are different realities. There is no truth at all to that sing-song childhood chant, 'seeing is believing;' You do not believe what you see; you know it. You have sensible experience of it, and you just *know*. What you do not, or cannot see, you can still believe (and thus, know) on evidence given to you by another—a trustworthy other. In this case, you do not see, but you surely know.

For me personally, faith is indeed the act by which I entrust myself to God. I don't have 'faith in the future,' for example. My faith is in God. One of the challenges to my faith is what John Courtney Murray many years ago identified as "atheism by distraction." This is not classic atheism, but in the face of the achievements of science, technology, and engineering which meet my needs for water, food, healthcare, and national security, I am distracted away from a sense of my dependence on God—hence, I become an atheist by distraction.

For me, the remedy for this is an abiding sense of gratitude. Building a spirituality based on gratitude is one way, by God's grace, of deepening my faith.

All of us can take an inventory of that for which we should be grateful, and then let an attitude of gratitude—the awareness of being indebted to God, who is the giver of all that we possess—get to work within us to quietly deepen our faith.

That might not be such a bad way that we can now use to carry forward the spirit of what Pope Benedict had in mind in calling for a Year of Faith.

PUTTING THE SOCIAL MEDIA TO WORK FOR THE REVITALIZATION OF THE CHURCH

Additional implications of the Year of Faith can be found in a little noticed engine of progress at work in President Obama's successful reelection campaign in 2012. Quietly and effectively at work under the overall supervision of Jim Messina, the campaign director, was a whole team of people, including a 'digital director,' a 'chief digital strategist,' a 'chief technology officer,' a 'deputy digital director,' a 'chief analytics officer,' a 'director of front-end development,' a 'director of digital products,' a 'digital analytics director,' and a 'web developer.'

What *Business Week Magazine* described as the Obama team's "maniacal focus on personal data" yielded millions of voters. It also, in the words of digital director Teddy Goff, "raised more money online this time than last time, had more donors, more volunteers, registered more people to vote online, and did all kinds of revolutionary stuff through Facebook and Twitter."

Corporations and ordinary businesses certainly took notice. The day after the election they were swooping in to hire these digital magicians for commercial, not political, purposes.

I can't help but wonder whether or not the United States Conference of Catholic Bishops, or any of the Dioceses that face declining Sunday Mass attendance or empty seats in Catholic schools, asked themselves if there is a lesson there waiting to be learned by a Church that is not doing well at all in the numbers game.

Introduction of the so-called social media into the national political campaign in 2012 made a world of difference. "Once all the votes are counted," reports *Business Week* (November 26, 2012), "about 1.25 million more young people will have supported Obama in 2012 than in 2008, when his ability to turn out 18-to-24-year-olds was hailed as revolutionary."

The success of the Catholic Church with that same age group is anything but impressive. It is surely time for managers of Diocesan and parish affairs to be talking to the techies in search of answers to the question of how to reach not only the young, but also the not-so-young, who are no longer showing up on Sundays. This is a crisis which must be met in new and creative ways.

Why not set up data centers in seminaries where computer-savvy young men are receiving classical preparation to serve congregations that may or may not be there by the time today's seminarians are ordained? Are computer-literate young lay men and women being encouraged to bring the new media into chancery offices and pastoral centers? This all points to something distinctively new which might be incorporated into the 'New Evangelization' that has been struggling to emerge since Pope Benedict XVI introduced the Year of Faith.

My faith is in God, of course, but also in the young who, I believe, God would want us to welcome technology into Diocesan decision-making circles. They can bring to the table knowledge of the social media, and offer suggestions as to how those tools can be put to work for the revitalization of the Catholic faith community.

Businesses are now doing this routinely. This is another page that the Church should be lifting from the business playbook.

WHAT WAS NEW IN THE 'NEW EVANGELIZATION?'

In making the announcement for the Year of Faith, Benedict called for a 'New Evangelization.' I've read and re-read his apostolic letter "Porta Fidei" (the Gate of Faith), which carried the announcement, and I've questioned a lot of people in an effort to discover what might be new about this New Evangelization. If you want to look at the letter, you can find it at http://www.vatican.va/holy_father/benedict_xvi/motu_proprio/documents.

The Year of Faith began on the 50th anniversary of the opening of the Second Vatican Council. Remarkably, this same date also marked the 20th anniversary of the publication of the Catechism of the Catholic Church. Hence, the documents of Vatican II and the Catechism (both referenced by Pope Benedict) might be presumed to be sources for discovery of what is new in the New Evangelization. Indeed, the Holy Father seemed to be suggesting that it is desirable for all Catholics to review those source documents again; perhaps for many that will mean seeing them for the first time.

The Year of Faith began with a Synod of Bishops in Rome. Pope Benedict gave that meeting a theme, namely, "The New Evangelization for the Transmission of the Christian Faith." Presumably, the bishops would be talking to one another about ways and means of getting the message across. The message is old, of course, as old as the Gospels. But the transmission—the delivery system, like an automobile transmission—has to be replaced or renewed. It just isn't working now. At least, that's how the Pope appeared to view the situation.

The content has been in place for centuries, but the delivery system needs attention. That problem is still with us.

Attention must be paid to the pulpit, the lecture hall, our publishing houses, and the new media—especially the Internet—if the delivery system is going to be improved. Any parish that doesn't have a library or website should set one up. Any Diocese that wants to reach the baptized but un-catechized should be working now on a good strategic plan. It won't be necessary to re-invent the wheel. But it will be necessary to find out what works and where it is working, and then put it to work locally.

Pastors would do well, if they did not do so during the Year of Faith, to convene committees both to contribute concepts and derive ideas from what began to emerge once the Year of Faith got underway. Parish-based committees made up of journalists, teachers, religious educators, tech- and media-savvy younger folks, marketing people, and anyone else who wants to participate can dot the Diocesan landscape and form a national network ready to implement the 'New Evangelization.'

This did not happen to any noticeable extent during the Year of Faith. But we have a new papacy now, and a great deal of fresh and emerging ideas. If parish committees do their job, the mechanism should be in place for something new to start to move.

The salt has all but lost its savor. Restoring it is what the 'New Evangelization' hoped to achieve. It is never too late for that to happen.

Chapter Five

FACING UP TO THE CRISIS IN CATHOLIC MODERNITY

There's a book of scholarly essays that I warmly recommend to all Catholics—lay and clergy, hierarchy and lowerarchy. It is co-edited by two lay Catholics—both retired historians—Michael Lacey and Francis Oakley. It is titled, *The Crisis of Authority in Catholic Modernity* (Oxford University Press, 2011).

In his prologue, Michael Lacey identifies the issue that looms the largest in the inquiring minds of ordinary practicing Catholics today as "the developing crisis of ecclesiastical authority, particularly the teaching authority of the clerical hierarchy, the magisterium." He adds that the "quiet insistence upon thinking for oneself is the chief characteristic of Catholic modernity."

How are the 'thinking-for-themselves' modern Catholics and their appointed hierarchical leaders getting along? That's another way of pointing out that, without reception, a magisterium can hardly be said to teach, and another way of asking how a teaching Church learns. It also suggests that if authority becomes authoritarian, it can expect a collision sooner rather than later with modernity.

Evidence of the collision abounds in surveys of Catholic opinion and practice in recent years.

Lacey and Oakley present a dozen essays that burrow into all of this. They review Church history, explore Church teaching, examine Catholic practice, and assess both continuity and discontinuity in official Catholic teaching through the years. Issues that unite, divide, confuse and comfort modern Catholics are examined in the wake of the Second Vatican Council which ended in 1965. These issues are also examined in the light of the twin affirmation of papal primacy and papal infallibility delivered by the First Vatican Council in 1869-70. How does collegiality fit in with primacy? How should bishops be working together, now with one another and with the Pope, in exercising their collective teaching authority? What does infallibility really mean?

I agree with Lacey's assertion that "The search is for authority without authoritarianism, clergy without clericalism, and acknowledgment from those who hold formal powers that the spirit of unity that must ever be fostered does not entail strict uniformity of thought and behavior."

This book is offered to thinking Catholics who are interested in pursuing this search. It will be most helpful to shepherd-leaders who want to serve.

In his epilogue to this collection, Francis Oakley points to the "sobering fact that between 1967 and 2007 almost a quarter of those Americans who were raised Catholic have voted with their feet and quietly left the Church, while, it should be added, a clear majority of those who remained have not only abandoned the practice of auricular confession but patently declined to 'receive' the papal teaching on artificial birth control that Paul VI in 1968 reaffirmed so forcefully in Humanae Vitae."

This book not only acknowledges the presence of all the elephants in the room, it provides a broad framework, with the needed historical perspective, to examine this crisis thoughtfully. Those concerned about the crisis will agree that the teaching Church must become a listening Church, that room must be made for humility in Church governance, that attention must be paid to "Assessing the Education of Priests and Lay Ministers" (the chapter title of an excellent contribution by Katarina Schuth), and that the time is now to face up to the problem of authority and its limits in our Church.

We are a people of hope, we Catholics We will only fail ourselves if we refuse to face our present reality—the genuine crisis of authority in the Church. We also know that by the power of the Spirit we can work our way through this crisis toward a better future.

THE CATHOLIC PARISH IN THE 21st CENTURY

Villanova University's Center for the Study of Church Management and Business Ethics celebrated its tenth anniversary in 2014 by hosting a one-day seminar on campus in cooperation with CARA (the Center for Applied Research in the Apostolate) which marked its fiftieth year of service to the Church. CARA has been in various locations in the Washington, DC area over the years; it is now a free-standing entity at, but not of, Georgetown University.

As those familiar with university life know, any academic with a good idea, a letterhead, and a file cabinet can initiate a center for the study of just about anything. Chuck Zech, a professor of economics at Villanova, saw the need a decade earlier for research into what might be called 'best practices' that would enable Church organizations to function more efficiently, ethically, and productively. He started conducting that research. He also convinced the Dean of the Villanova School of Business that there is a market for a Master's Degree program (predominantly online) in Church management. Both activities—instructional and research—are underway; in 2013 the Center added Business Ethics to its program.

Full disclosure prompts me to mention that I serve on the Villanova Center's advisory council; in that capacity I was invited to participate in the joint seminar celebrating the Center's tenth and CARA's fiftieth anniversary. Under the heading of "The Catholic Parish in the 21st Century," these two rather well-kept secrets in the life of the American Church provide a stimulating program for about 200 Church types, clergy and lay, on the challenges and opportunities facing the Church in the immediate future.

Melissa Cidade, of CARA, gave an enlightening presentation on the demographics and diversity associated with the American Church today. Her colleague Mark Gray addressed the challenges and opportunities associated with Catholic schools and the sacraments. He prompted me to wonder, in view of the downturn in Catholic elementary school enrollment, whether any Catholics in future years will realize that Guardian Angels are not citizen patrols, but rather celestial companions who can be relied upon for protection and guidance. ("Ever this day be at my side to light and guard, to rule and guide. . . ")

Jesuit Father Thomas Gaunt, CARA's executive director outlined CARA's approach to research design and financial support. Professor Zech gave specifics about stewardship and the uses and abuses of parish finances. He had predicted not long after the clergy sexual abuse scandal rocked the Church in 2001 that disclosures of financial fraud and embezzlement would soon surface as a troubling issue. He was right.

Keynoting the conference was Fr. Michael White, a pastor in suburban Baltimore, who has tripled weekend attendance at his parish. He highlighted three 'M's' as keys to growth for the Catholic parish in the years ahead. They are: music, message (the homily), and ministers (welcoming ministers when worshipers arrive and parking-lot facilitators who ease their arrivals). It struck me that a forth 'M' needs attention—the meal. As I mentioned before in this book, we are there on Sundays to remember the Lord in the breaking of the Bread. We become one in theOone loaf and the One cup which are ours to share. We need more effective catechesis on the meaning of that meal. No question that there is need for better music and improved homilies. But without deeper understanding of the Eucharist, we could wind up with mega-parishes and malnourished parishioners.

THE PROBLEM OF PREACHING

At their November 2012 semi-annual meeting in Baltimore, the U.S. bishops gave overwhelming approval to a document titled "Preaching the Mystery of Faith: The Sunday Homily." It was the first time in 30 years that they addressed the issue of the quality of preaching in our nation's parishes.

They didn't say so explicitly, but the bishops seem to think that we are losing the game in the pulpit, and the people (those who are still showing up!) are looking for and deserving of much better preaching. As a friend put it to me not long ago, here in the U.S. "we have Saturday Night Live and Sunday morning dead." We can do better. And the bishops are now saying we must.

Their document says that "the homily is intended to establish a 'dialogue' between the sacred Biblical texts and the Christian life of the hearer." I would make that same point in different words. I would say that the homily is intended to be an extension of the proclamation of the Scripture texts that are part of every Mass. That proclamation should be filtered through the faith experience of the homilist, and then matched up with the faith experience of the people in the pews.

On the floor of the bishops' meeting while the preaching document was being discussed, Bishop Ricardo Ramirez of Las Cruces, New Mexico, pleaded for an amendment that would urge Catholics to make an extra effort to listen to heavily-accented foreign-born priests in order to grasp their message. He pointed out that "they have wisdom" and are "inspired by the Holy Spirit." Perhaps the heavy-accented preachers should be encouraged to write their homilies out, in English of course, and have them reproduced and available in the pews so that willing worshippers can read and understand their inspiring words.

Similarly, pastors might be encouraged to have acoustical checks run on their sound systems and require auditions for all lectors in order to guarantee that the Scripture readings are proclaimed audibly and clearly so that all can hear.

This continues to be a critically important issue for the Church. That's why the bishops addressed it. It remains to be seen what impact their document will have on parishes, seminaries, and training programs for deacons and lectors.

THE PARISH AS 'THIRD PLACE'

Third place is a sociological category which marks the next most important living space, after home and workplace, for most of us. I'm not talking about winners and losers when I refer to third place; I'm talking about human connectedness. I'm raising the question because I think it is important for pastors to see that there is a lot of work to be done in making their parishes a 'third place' magnet in the lives of their parishioners.

We connect primarily in the home. In order to make a living, we connect in the workplace. But there is a lot more to life than home and work and that *more*—as in the case of family life and work life—is usually associated with connecting to others in some identifiable place.

For many, the 'third place' is the club, or entertainment complex, or some cultural or recreational center. It could even be the local barber shop.

John Mackey, co-CEO of Whole Foods Market, boasts of establishing tap rooms inside his stores as a third place for customers. Beer on tap is available for immediate consumption there in the middle of the store. "The new venue was hugely successful from the day it opened, with very strong sales and high profit margins. It turned out that customers identify Whole Foods Market (as they do Starbucks) as a 'third place'... where they enjoy hanging out." (*Conscious Capitalism*, Harvard Business School Press, p. 248).

Typically, a parish has no pull on the loyalties of parishioners except for weekend worship, although the parish does have the potential to provide socialization—a sense of community—as well as gathering and meeting space for a variety of activities that can make lives fuller and more meaningful.

Church planners have to begin thinking of how the space under their control—the physical space that they own—can be used not only for meaningful liturgies, but also to attract members of their faith community to a fuller experience of social life. Some have parochial schools that add vitality to the place Monday through Friday. All could have libraries with associated lectures and discussion groups. Some have 'job seekers' support groups.

Others have sports leagues, pot luck suppers, dances, young adult groups, child care, adult day care, and a variety of other activities that go well beyond the after-Mass coffee-and-donut gatherings on Sunday mornings.

But none of this will work if the people have no desire to come together. They won't come together if they don't know one another. They will surely not come together unless they are summoned out of their isolation in creative ways. This will not happen without an on-the-scene presence of welcoming volunteers. Hence, pastoral planning has to begin with the people. What do they want? Who will lead? Who will open the doors and turn out the lights?

The pastor surely cannot do it all. But only the pastor can initiate a strategy for providing a 'third place' option in his underutilized space for those who are looking for company and something to do. He'll be surprised to find how many fit that description and are already registered on his parish rolls.

Chapter Six

FEWER LABORERS FOR A GROWING HARVEST

Over the centuries, men and women of faith, generosity, and zeal saw the great need for laborers to bring in the harvest which Jesus spoke about (Matthew 9: 37). They offered their services to the Church by becoming priests and religious who, like their Master, realized that they were on this Earth "not to be servod, but to serve, and to give their lives as a ransom for many" (Matthew 20:28).

There has been such a multiplication of religious orders, communities and congregations of men and women throughout the history of the Church that Catholics often joke that only God knows how many there actually have been. But their numbers are now declining. There are fewer priests and religious today than there were a generation or even two ago. So the question about the availability of laborers to bring in the harvest is very much on the Catholic mind, although it should be a concern for all.

An August 21, 2011 headline in *The New York Times* caught my eye: "Nuns, a 'Dying Breed,' Fade from Leadership

Roles at Catholic Hospitals.'" Here is the opening paragraph of that story: "When Sister Mary Jean Ryan entered the convent as a young nurse in 1960, virtually every department of every Catholic hospital was run by a nun, from pediatrics to dietary to billing. After her retirement on July 31 [2011] as the chief executive of one of the country's largest networks of Catholic hospitals, only 11 nuns remained among her company's more than 22,000 employees, and none were administrators."

Ponder the implications of those numbers as you consider the second paragraph of the news story, which ran under a St. Louis dateline: "For SSM [Sisters of St. Mary] Health Care, a $4.2 billion enterprise that evolved from the work of five German nuns who arrived here in 1872, Sister Mary Jean's departure after 25 years as the company's first chief executive marks a poignant passing. The gradual transition from religious to lay leadership, which has been changing the face of Catholic healthcare for decades, is now nearly complete."

From five immigrant nuns 140 years ago to a 22,000 employee healthcare system in 2011 is quite a transition! What might five nuns decide to do today, if they wanted to serve God's people? Where might one find five committed, venturesome, Catholic women who will band together to undertake such work today? Not in Sister Mary Jean's religious community. It, according to *The New York Times* story, "has dwindled to about 100 from a peak of more than 500. Most moved out of their convent last year and into a retirement and nursing home. There has not been an initiate [novice] for 25 years, and several years ago the sisters reluctantly stopped looking."

Is God still calling young men and women to religious life and related healthcare, educational, and social ministry? I think so, but I don't know that every existing religious order can count on a continuing flow of recruits. God is calling lay persons to religious life. Some of the religious orders have to adapt to new circumstances. Some will cease to exist. Some new orders will have to emerge to meet new needs.

The spectacle of happy men and women doing useful work will continue to attract the generous young to religious life. The sight of great fields of human need awaiting harvest will be there for potential harvesters to see. The question is: *Will they respond to the call?*

THE PRIEST SHORTAGE

If you walk along with Jesus by the Sea of Galilee, where you find him in Matthew 4:18, you will see Simon Peter and Simon's brother Andrew. They are fisherman and, as Jesus walks by, they are casting their nets into the sea. And Jesus said to them, "Come after me, and I will make you fishers of men." This is a call to discipleship. This is a call to all men and women in all stages of life. "Come," he says to every believer—to you and me today—"come and walk along with me," says Jesus, "come follow me."

Pause for a moment, here with Jesus, Peter, and Andrew, and open your eyes to the scene and your ears to the words. Then, taking the opportunity occasioned by this particular passage in Matthew's Gospel, try as best you can to open your mind to the question of the status and supply of priests in the Church in the United States today. The call which you hear in this Gospel passage is not explicitly or exclusively a call to ordained priesthood. It is a call to discipleship. But some disciples are called to priesthood, and it is to that call that I want to focus on here.

Dean Hoge, the late sociologist of religion who taught at The Catholic University of America, was a Presbyterian layman who studied for about 20 years what he typically referred to as 'the priest shortage' in the American Catholic Church. Not everyone would agree, despite the clear evidence of declining numbers, that there is a shortage of priests in the U.S.—some would say there is just a shortage of celebrants! Others would argue that God wills this to be a new age of opportunity for lay ministry; fewer clergy are needed. Or they will assert that if the Catholic Church ordained women, or admitted married men to Holy Orders, there would be more than enough ordained pastors to tend to the needs of the flock.

Say what you think about this situation as you walk along in your imagination with Jesus, Peter and Andrew; at least say it to yourself. Try to imagine what they—Jesus, Andrew, and Peter—might want to say to you about the priest shortage in America today.

I certainly hope Christ will tap on the shoulder of some modern Peters and Andrews, and invite them to drop their nets (Internets or any other kind), and free themselves up to follow him, to answer in the affirmative when he says, "Come after me, and I will make you fishers of men."

Some readers might wince at the phrase, "fishers of men." I feel certain that if Jesus were speaking today, he would surely say "fishers of men and women," fishers or servants of all humankind. Here with us in a modern technological society, he would be looking for generous and competent Peters and Andrews in a world not limited to fishing nets, but a modern world of telecommunications and broadcast networks, a commercial world of supply networks, a scientific world of information networks, a world of political networks, an interdependent, interconnected world of human beings all in need of Salvation in and through the redemptive sacrifice of Christ. As we all know, Christ chooses to work the Salvation of the world though the ministry of disciples, humans like you and me, some of whom he wants to serve as priests.

Are the Andrea's and Petra's of our modern Catholic community not included in this call? All—-men and women alike—-are called to discipleship, to follow Christ. But are the Andrea's and Petra's excluded from the call to ordained priestly ministry in our Church today? Yes, they are now. Will that last forever? Who can say? Surely, no one can say with certainty that they will never be called to priesthood since, as we all know, "nothing is impossible with God" (Luke 1:37). But not for now.

Nor are married men now called to ordination in our Church, although that may change in the nearer term. For now, however, we know that our Church admits to the ranks of the ordained only men committed to celibacy. What might Jesus, Andrew, and Peter be saying about this as you walk along in conversation with them today?

I can speculate on what they might be saying, but I don't know for sure. I do know this, however, Andrew and Peter, two of the pillars on which our Church was founded, would surely want to see the priesthood continue on in service to the human community in our modern times. If this is to happen, the Church needs priests. I feel certain that Peter and Andrew, and Christ himself, would urge patience on us all as Christ invites some few to give themselves in freedom to ordained ministry in and for the people of God.

Dean Hoge would surely tell us, if he were here today, that his research shows celibacy to be a major obstacle encountered by young men when they face up to the question of whether or not priesthood is their calling. Lifetime commitment to ordained priesthood is another obstacle. So is the exclusion of women from Holy Orders. Anyone who surveys the young to get at their thinking on this issue will agree that these three are major obstacles. These are institutional barriers, if you will, matters that have to be attended to—not necessarily changed, but given careful consideration—by a listening, reflective Church that is obedient to the will of God.

Meanwhile, all of us—men and women, young and old (but young men, in particular)—have to give this question the attention it deserves (as Andrew and Peter were attentive to this vocational issue, and responsive, when they heard Jesus say, "Come after me.").

Jesus said to Peter and Andrew, "'Come after me, and I will make you fishers of men.' At once they left their nets and followed him. He walked along from there and saw two other brothers, James, the son of Zebedee, and his brother John. They were in a boat, with their father Zebedee, mending their nets. He called them, and immediately they left their boat and their father and followed him. He went around all of Galilee, teaching in their synagogues, proclaiming the Gospel of the Kingdom, and curing every disease and illness among the people."

They followed him. And there lies a lesson for us all. Note that he invited them to become part of a movement; he had no construction plans for the building of a monument! All the more reason why we should be wary of letting that movement harden into a monument.

Chapter Seven

TOWARD A BALANCED
CHRISTIAN LIFE

I have a long-time friend whose name is Martha, although everyone calls her Martie. She tells me that the Gospel story of Martha and Mary was a familiar one around her home as she was growing up with two sisters with whom she frequently debated the fairness of the allocation of household chores, particularly the task of cleaning up after dinner.

Her brothers were mute auditors of these discussions back in the days when male members of the family where not held responsible for kitchen cleanup. But the relative responsibilities of Martha and Mary, about which Jesus had some interesting things to say, were and still are topics of conversation in many Catholic families.

It is interesting to note that the famous Dutch artist Rembrandt (1606 – 1669), whose paintings of the "Face of Jesus" were exhibited in the Philadelphia Museum of Art in 2011, chose the Biblical story of Martha and Mary as the subject for several pieces of his pen-and-brown-ink-on-paper religious art. In one instance, he purposely smears or "washes," as the art critics say, the figure of Martha, as if to highlight her harried activity in contrast to the clear ink depiction of Jesus and Martha's sister, Mary, sitting quietly at the table. In at least two of his renderings of this Biblical scene, included in the "Face of Jesus" exhibit, Rembrandt has Mary reading a book as if to add studiousness to the contemplative dimension of her character.

The story is familiar. Martha was the one who welcomed Jesus to their home. Mary, her sister, seemed not to notice that Martha "was busy with all the details of hospitality." Famously, Martha spoke up to Jesus and complained, "Lord, are you not concerned that my sister has left me all alone to do the household tasks? Tell her to help me." To Martha's surprise, I suspect, Jesus replied by reminding her that there are two sides to the Christian life—the active and the contemplative—and that Mary "has chosen the better [part] and shall not be deprived of it."

Over the centuries, there's been no little debate in the Catholic world about the relative merits of the active life over the vocation to contemplative life. Who has the higher calling—the active Maryknoll missionary, or the prayerful Trappist monk? The Carmelite nun in her monastery, or the Sister of Mercy in her hospital? The Catholic lay teacher, or the classroom Christian Brother?

Reflection on the story of Martha and Mary presents all of us with an opportunity to give some thought to balance in our lives. We tend to neglect the demands of the quiet side in favor of the hyperactive being-busy-about-a-lot-of-things side of our lives. We want to be on the move. We want to be busy about a lot of things. In other words, we want to be like Martha.

But Jesus says that Mary chose the better part—to sit at his feet, to quietly contemplate, to listen. If Rembrandt is to be believed, Jesus expects those who would follow him to read a book or two and to get their minds engaged.

The trouble with the world, someone once remarked, is that most of the active people never think, and most of the thinkers never act. We need both—thought and action—in all areas of life. In our contemporary Christian world, however, we seem to be letting busyness and all sorts of distractions crowd out the contemplative; that is a particular problem for the young.

TRYING TO UNDERSTAND THE YOUNG

Elders in America always seem at a loss to explain what is going on in the minds of the young. It is worth taking time to try to understand younger minds and motives, particularly as we wonder about the young responding to the call to discipleship and worry about the young losing interest in the practice of their faith.

Sometimes a good book can be helpful in investigating a question like this. I came across one recently, and I warmly recommend it: "Lost in Transition: The Dark Side of Emerging Adulthood" by sociologist Christian Smith and several of his colleagues at the University of Notre Dame. Technically, an 'emerging adult' is between the ages of 18 and 29; Smith and his co-authors narrow that age span and make it 18 to 23, the typical age spread for a college student body.

If you want to better understand what makes today's college students tick, read this book. They have a lot of good things going for them, but they also have a dark side that deserves attention on the part of parents, educators, pastors and anyone interested in the future of America. Attention must be paid, say these researchers, because the dark side characteristics they have discovered are not simply going to disappear as this age cohort grows older. Moreover, the lives and experiences of youth reflect the condition of the adult world that has produced them.

The experience of American life between the ages of 18 and 30 has dramatically changed. What are the indicators of present troubles that raise concerns for the future?

First, there's been great growth in higher education, not just college but graduate and professional schools, as well. Of itself, of course, that's a positive development. But it represents a new, lengthening-out phase in the life course inasmuch as many now continue to be students into their late twenties and early thirties. Second, is the delay in marriage for many American youth, and the related problems of cohabitation and thin interpersonal commitments. Third, economic change at home and abroad has undermined stable, life-long careers, resulting in economic insecurity that lasts well into adulthood. A fourth change is the willingness of parents to have young adult children live, for economic reasons, at home throughout their 20's and into their 30's. That is not all bad, of course, but it generates an extended search for identity and autonomy in the young. Fifth, over the past five decades birth control technologies have become more accessible and effective, thus disconnecting sexual intercourse from reproduction in the American mind. This raises questions about the future of the family. The sixth troubling indicator is a striking return of individualism accompanied by a rise in moral relativism within the American mind.

The book's chapter titles stake out the range of analysis covered: "Morality Adrift," "Captive to Consumerism," "Intoxication's 'Fake Feeling of Happiness,'" "The Shadow Side of Sexual Liberation," and "Civic and Personal Disengagement."

The prospect of moral nomads addicted to consumption, inclined to binge drinking, and for whom sexual liberation has meant hurt, confusion, and regrets, along with disengagement from the political process, should be enough to call for attention and a national response.

These researchers conclude that "almost all emerging adults today are either apathetic, uninformed, distrustful, disempowered, or, at most, only marginally interested when it comes to politics and public life." Cause for concern? You bet.

Read the book and try to figure out what can be done to trim back emerging adulthood to a shorter span while attending, as any responsible society should, to the dilution of values exhibited in all too many young adults today.

Chapter Eight

WHAT DOES IT MEAN TO BE A CATHOLIC IN THE UNITED STATES TODAY?

On the Sunday before Pope Benedict XVI arrived in the United States in April 2008, the *Philadelphia Inquirer* ran a positive editorial of welcome and took the occasion to raise an interesting question: "What does it mean to be a Catholic in the U.S. today?" That's a question worthy of consideration right here.

All Catholics should be reflecting on that question—individually, to be sure, but also with others. It is an important question and the range of possible answers is wide. No one of us can say it all in just a few paragraphs, but each of us should try to form a reasonably concise reply.

I would begin by saying that being a Catholic today in the U.S. means being a person of commitment within a community.

The community, of course, is the Church, with the Pope as a leader, teacher, and symbol of unity. But even in the

Church we find ourselves in other communities. There is the conjugal community for so many (marriage and the family). There are celibate religious communities for some, and there are those who remain single yet still belong to families and relate to others in a variety of helping relationships.

Countless Catholics identify with other communities in their workplaces and in leisure hours, where they are known as Catholic and where they witness to the truths of their Catholic faith.

The commitment associated with being a Catholic (remember, I said that being Catholic means being a person of commitment within a community) is, first and foremost, to Jesus Christ. We are Christians. Catholic life is Christo-centric. It is both nourished and celebrated in the Eucharist. The community within which this commitment is most evident is a worshipping community who remembers the Lord in the breaking of the Bread (Acts 20). Being Catholic means being a part of all of that through both Word (Scripture) and Sacrament (Catholics count seven of these). Being Catholic also means having special reverence and respect for Mary because she is the mother of Jesus.

Scripture introduces the Catholic to law (the Ten Commandments, as well as the law of love). Scripture, as proclamation, invites the response of faith. Catholic faith, in search of deeper understanding, applies intellect to the content of Scripture in the exercise of Catholic theology. Theology attempts explanation, as contrasted with proclamation, and therefore develops new understandings (development of doctrine) over the years. Hence, being a Catholic means being lifted through life on the wings of both faith and reason.

ON THE WINGS OF FAITH AND REASON

Being Catholic also means being committed to the care of those in need. Those three 'C's'—commitment, community, and care—say a lot about what it means to be a Catholic in the U.S. today.

To be a Catholic today certainly means to be with, and for, the poor. It means to promote peace and justice, to protect and respect human life from conception to natural death, and to care for the earth. Stewardship, in the Catholic view, extends to the care and cultivation of one's personal gifts of body and mind.

For Catholics, sexuality is to be expressed within the context of community (marriage and family, and preparation for both) and permanent commitment (fidelity). Sexual pleasure is purposeful in keeping with God's plan for Creation. Similarly, material possessions are to be managed within the context of community (ownership may be private, but use is common) as well as commitment to stewardship, service, and the good of others.

Being Catholic in the U.S. today means having freedom, responsibility, and accountability—freedom in the Holy Spirit, responsibility for one's free choices, and accountability for one's actions and the use of one's talents A reflective reading of Scripture reminds the Catholic that

1—"you shall know the truth and the truth will set you free" (John 8:32); 2—that each is indeed his or her "brother's [and sister's] keeper" (Genesis 4:9); and 3—that all of us will have to give an account before God in keeping with the judgment scene portrayed in Matthew 25. Earlier in Matthew's Gospel (5:1-12), the Beatitudes provide a summary of Catholic convictions.

Finally, to be a Catholic means to live in gratitude for all of God's gifts, a gratitude that provides a firm foundation for moral obligation. We present ourselves as 'much obliged' (grateful) before God on Sundays. On all seven days of the week we consider ourselves obliged, as well, to love one another as Christ has loved us. There you have a relatively concise answer to an extraordinarily important question. Try your own hand at shaping the answer that lies there in your own mind and heart. What does it mean to you to be a Catholic today?

Chapter Nine

IS THERE A LINK BETWEEN FORGIVENESS AND JUSTICE?

A lawyer friend once asked me whether forgiveness can, in any way, be a form of justice. I think it can, but the relationship is not easy to explain. It is worth the effort however, because the relationship lies close to the heart of Christianity.

The healing power of forgiveness cannot be overemphasized. Whether given or received, and regardless of whether it comes from God or another human being, forgiveness heals.

Jim Wallis, the pastor of Sojourners Community in Washington, D.C., and longtime editor of *Sojourners Magazine*, says that "the idea of forgiveness often seems abstract and 'religious' in an otherworldly kind of way. But, in fact, forgiveness is very practical and necessary for human life on the planet to survive.... When we refuse to forgive, the cycle of vengeance, retaliation, and violence just escalates.... It is only genuine forgiveness that breaks the cycle of destruction and opens up new possibilities."

The Sermon on the Mount, which contains some firm instruction against retaliation, addressed the issue of forgiveness in the context of worship. Your refusal to forgive would make you unworthy to stand before the altar. "If you bring your gift to the altar and there recall that your brother or sister has anything against you, leave your gift at the altar, go first to be reconciled with your brother or sister, and then come and offer your gift" (Matthew 5:23-24).

We Christians should measure our performance in this regard against the standard embodied in the Lord's Prayer: "Forgive us our trespasses, as we forgive those who trespass against us." Realize that, in making this prayer, we are asking to be forgiven on a contingent basis. We are declaring ourselves to be willing to be forgiven only if we forgive others. This is a remarkable standard. No one is perfect, of course, but no one can dodge that standard; it will be there to challenge us every day of our lives.

It takes a large-hearted person to decide to forgive; the act of forgiving enlarges the heart of the forgiver.

Forgiveness fastens friendships. Anyone interested in contributing to the return of loyalty to everyday life might simply look for opportunities to forgive. Anyone who can count should take a moment to calculate, in practical terms, the value of the lesson that is available to everyone in these words of Merle Shain: "There is no way to hate another that does not cost the hater, no way to remain unforgiving without maiming yourself."

Most of us are familiar with Alexander Pope's dictum: "To err is human, to forgive, divine," and we've often heard that it is wise to "forgive and forget," although Shakespeare put that proposition the other way around on the lips of King Lear: "Pray you now, forget and forgive."

None of us will ever be divine, but we can imitate divinity in forgiving. We may never be able to forget, but we can act as if we have forgotten whenever we forgive from the heart. In either case, true forgiveness is the restorative measure, the transforming decision that puts you on a brand new page. And that, it seems to me, has to have some relationship to justice.

However you understand justice, it has to do with the promotion and protection of right relationships. Biblical justice refers to right relationships with God. Economic justice refers to right relationships with others in the marketplace. Legal justice looks to right relationships under the law. Forgiveness, it seems to me, is an instrument capable of forging all right relationships. So, with the possibility of forgiveness, there is always reason to hope.

WALKING IN HOPE

About 400 years ago, the Welsh-born English poet George Herbert expressed the encouraging idea that anyone "who walks in hope dances without music." Most of us have to make it through life without the benefit of background music. Whether you walk or dance, you make your way each day by even-paced measures without the tempo-enhancing encouragement of violins and trumpets.

For many years, the movies have been offering lessons about life that are cleverly (and often deceptively) wrapped in background music. Characters in the films have music to intensify their emotional highs, warn them (and the audience) of impending danger, or accelerate their slide into deeper despair. In those rare moments of emotional intensity when the music stops, the viewer is left in a suspended state of watching and waiting, trying (often uncomfortably) to figure out what will happen next.

Real life is different. You can make your own movies, so to speak, by imagining what, and why, and how you will do what you are going to do today and in all your tomorrows. But you have to choose the attitude—the inner silent state of mind—that will accompany you (and serve as your "accompaniment") along the way. If you want to walk in hope, you have to choose to do so.

Hope is not to be confused with optimism, which focuses always on 'the best.' 'Optimizing' opportunities and achieving 'optimal' outcomes might be 'optimistically' regarded as part of 'the best' in the 'best of all worlds.' That is not the way it is with hope. Hope is a great deal closer to the human heart—hesitant or stout, weak or strong—and to the ground on which the have-a-heart person walks (or dances!).

I have no idea when the word 'hopefully' rose to the prominent place of misapplication that it now enjoys within the American vernacular. This adverb means "in a happily expectant way." If used correctly, it would describe a personal condition similar to the mood conveyed in expressions like "proudly announce," or "gladly welcome." The misapplied "hopefully" (e.g., "Hopefully, we will hear from them soon.") really means, "It is to be hoped that..."

This is more than a simple grammatical quibble. Most of the people I hear punctuating their conversations with the word 'hopefully' do not give all that much evidence of being all that hopeful!

Hope is the pillar of the world. It is a theological virtue and its object is always God. Because of it, the person of hope is a lot stronger than he or she might think. The novelist John Updike once wrote, "God is a bottomless encouragement to our faltering and frightened being."

As the famous "Prayer of St. Francis" puts it, "Lord, make me an instrument of your peace . . . where there is despair, let me sow hope." So, be hopeful; just decide to let it happen. Let the experience of forgiveness serve as a foundation for your hope as you look forward—in hope—to the experience of death.

THE GRASP OF THE GRAVE

I've been attending a lot of funerals lately—high school and college classmates, longtime friends, close relatives. I've also been struck by references in Scripture to the fact of our mortality. Not surprising, I guess, given my age (I've been around since 1927!) and the fragility of life, but it does prompt me to ponder.

For example, these words from Psalm 89 jumped off the page of my Breviary and hit me between the eyes one recent morning, the day after I drove three hours each way to be there for the funeral of my nephew's mother-in-law: "What man can live and never see death? Who can save himself from the grasp of the grave?" No debate about the answer to both of those questions.

In that same morning prayer, I read: "Our life is over like a sigh, our span is seventy years, or eighty for those who are strong" (Psalm 90). Several of the recent funeral farewells I've participated in honored friends who were well into their eighties, some of them veterans of the Second World War and, as another friend remarked to me at the cemetery, "No one does it better than the Catholic Church and the U.S. Military," as the bugler played Taps, the flag was removed from covering the casket, folded carefully, and presented with a salute to the surviving spouse.

One of my recently deceased friends was an ex-Marine (some would insist that there is no such person—once a Marine, always a Marine), an avid rower, and an unusually loyal alumnus of his prep school. Many years after graduating, he led a successful effort to build a boat house for his high school alma mater's rowing program. After his death, the school honored his life by arranging for the members of that year's varsity eight to serve as pall bearers. They also hosted an after-funeral luncheon at the boat house with a ceremonial "row by" to show gratitude from healthy athletes who, of course, think they are immortal but will eventually discover that they, too, cannot escape the 'grasp of the grave.' The family of this former rower, knowing well his life-long devotion to his prep school, arranged that the metal vault into which his casket was inserted, when lowered into the grave, was painted in his high school's colors of crimson and gray! I've never seen that before!

But I have seen flowers, usually roses, distributed to mourners at the grave site with instructions to drop the flower on the casket with a parting prayer before leaving the cemetery. Very recently, I held a yellow rose at the graveside of lovely woman whose husband, children and grandchildren stood by listening as a friend recited the words, as he recalled them, of a poem Countee Cullen composed on the occasion of his grandmother's death:

> "This lovely flower fell to seed.
> Be gentle wind and rain.
> She held it as her dying creed
> That she would rise again."

And so she will. And so shall we who believe in Jesus, and know that because we believe in him we shall live with him forever. That is where forgiveness, justice, and hope all lead, thus making the 'grasp of the grave' a welcoming embrace.

www.ingramcontent.com/pod-product-compliance
Lightning Source LLC
LaVergne TN
LVHW051606080426
835510LV00020B/3155